T0196516

Haiku PUNmanship: Book Five

Paul Treatman

iUniverse, Inc.
New York   Bloomington

Copyright © 2010 by Paul Treatman

All rights reserved. No part of this book may be used or reproduced by any means, graphic, electronic, or mechanical, including photocopying, recording, taping or by any information storage retrieval system without the written permission of the publisher except in the case of brief quotations embodied in critical articles and reviews.

iUniverse books may be ordered through booksellers or by contacting:

iUniverse
1663 Liberty Drive
Bloomington, IN 47403
www.iuniverse.com
1-800-Authors (1-800-288-4677)

Because of the dynamic nature of the Internet, any Web addresses or links contained in this book may have changed since publication and may no longer be valid. The views expressed in this work are solely those of the author and do not necessarily reflect the views of the publisher, and the publisher hereby disclaims any responsibility for them.

ISBN: 978-1-4502-4510-4 (sc)
ISBN: 978-1-4502-4511-1 (ebook)

Printed in the United States of America

iUniverse rev. date: 09/15/2010

Acknowledgments

Thank you, Sylvia Rubin, your love and devotion are my raison d'être.

This little volume is my latest in a quintilogy (is there such a word?) of five books of haikus with a twist, the twist being the embedding of a pun in the haiku context.

HAIKU PUNmanship follows HAIKU PUNishment,, A HAIKU/ PUN FOR EVERYONE, MORE HAIKU FOR PUNSTERS, and HAIKUS FOR PUNSTERS (these titles listed in reverse chronological order).

My thanks for some punny suggestions go to Sylvia Rubin, Bernie Gutstadt, Linda Lemay, Dann Mann and Chuck Farber. In a sense, they have rewarded (or PUNished?) me for tolerating what I have inflicted upon them in recent years.

Dedication

To Abbe Jo and Jeffrey, Scott and Linda, Melissa and Bryon, Jennifer and Anthony; Elexa, Ava, Jake, Troy, and Anthony Jackson, any more great-grandchildren in the future.
And
To the cherished memory of
Elaine Treatman, who started it all.

Foreword

The haiku is a very old Japanese verse form that attempts to express cogently a thought in an economical three lines, five syllables in the first and third lines and seven syllables in the second line. The haiku has flowered in recent decades among poets and children nationwide.

In this book, as in my previous four, I have melded the haiku form with the pun - a form of humor considered lowly by many. Not me. I have always loved and used puns, especially when I wanted to get thrown out of parties that bored me.

Puns have been used by poets, including Shakespeare, even long before the haiku appeared. The pun is a word, phrase or expression that is play on words. The pun might be word with a double meaning within the context of the thought expressed. It might be a word by design almost sounds like another word different from the word that the listener or reader was expecting. It might be a two-word expression whose first letters have been deliberately transposed for a hopefully comic effect. Mrs. Malaprop's mindless malapropisms were also puns.

All of these haikus are mine. Most of the embedded puns are mine. I confess that a handful of embedded puns I swiped from the general domain and cyberspace. I wove the puns into haikus, a shotgun marriage that I pray will entertain you.

Paul Treatman

Lancelot: Your castle

Is well protected. Arthur

You said a moatful.

She asked her busy

Butcher for lamb and he gave

Her the cold shoulder.

Family auto

Trip to nudist camp, the kid

Asks: "Are we bare yet?"

Bark-eating creatures

Are lickin' the lichen and

Likin' the lickin'.

Childishly silly

For years, he finally reached

His adultery.

Inept staffer at

Service desk is sometimes called

Miss Information.

A political

Strategist often played on

A word and pundit.

He was such a cute

Little baby boy,

But now I see he gruesome.

Dad gulped so many

Vitamins that I would call

Him a pill poppa.

Bride throws her bouquet

To bridesmaids and thankfully

Becomes deflowered.

British diplomat

Enjoys an afternoon of

High tea and strumpets.

The new rock and roll

Group in the U.K. is known

As the Rolling Scones.

She felt if she had

Wed him, it would have been for

Better or for curse.

Football coach to the

Doctor: "I'm hurting, please check

My weak quarter back.."

Large sign seen on an

Italian bistro: Uncle

And Aunty Pasto.

He: "Let's take off

And marry." She: "I cantaloupe."

He: "Please honeydew."

Admiring Asian

Mystics, he travels East to

Study now and Zen.

Subterranean

Cache is where the buyer and

The cellar would meet.

If you forget when

Your friends will come for dinner,

Check your collender.

Punxsatauney Phil:

"I'd rather be a cold groundhog

Than a cold, ground, hog."

Limited vision

Hematologist always

Pokes my arm in vain.

Psychiatrist, quite

Disracted, often pays his

Few patients no mind.

Fishing contest, Lake

Michigan, men are carping

With one another.

Vice lord and girl friend

Buy huge blanket so they can

Smuggle together.

Some muscle building

Products that contain protein

Priced whey out of line.

Cowardly Lion

Beseeches Dorothy: "I must

Drink Chock Full O' Guts."

One attorney to

Another: "I'll give you a

Penny for your torts."

Commentator with

Foul mouth changes network to

Become Sirius.

Recent novel has

A dragon singing out, "Fangs

For the Memory."

Hypochondriac

Grandma, drunk, seeks attention

With lots of sham pain.

Tramp rides the rails in

New Jersey, claims

That any Hoboken do it.

Chinese recruit in

Army sits in the mess hall

And finds his chow fun.

Farm boy is jumping

Farm girl to farm girl, just

Loves sowing his groats.

Libido in a

Recession, he beds her

With blue stimulust pill.

Fisherman not, he

Cast his line anyway, just

For the halibut.

Male ducks refuse to

Congregate with female ducks,

"We are Orthoducks!"

Mosquito stings old

Gent, who cries out, "I hope it's

Not C-Nile virus!"

Wayward husband comes

Home late and does not offer

Any sexcuses.

Dry cleaner closes

Store for a day because of

Pressing business.

Tropical fish store

Closes shop when they see its

Business tanking.

His supply of meds

To relieve his itching cost

Him plenty of scratch.

Wheat crop fails, farmer

Laments: "My grain is giving

Me severe headaches."

Entomologist

Recommends slab of dry ice

To control incest.

Crocodile swallows

Brown rodent, thus enjoying

A chocolate mousse.

Jungle cat steals food

From mate, is accused as a

Crude, dirty cheetah.

Prices in the isles

Of the Caribbean are

A shine of the times.

Bird watchers, standing

On the corner and watching

All the gulls go by.

Dentist cruises to

Panama, feels he should be

Doing route canal.

Oh, say can you see

Radio City lights and

The Rockettes' red wear?

Researcher seeks funds

From the feds and just gets

Fifty dollar Grant.

He tasted chicken

And tried rib steak, both bad, then

Found the liverwurst.

Wife, hubby exchange

Recriminations as they

Stand there snide by snide.

Hotel guests find their

Bathrooms well appointed

And very commodious.

Electrician finds the

Wiring in old apartment

Extremely shocking.

I was so hot in

Florida I drank bottles

Of Pensacola.

Violinist fails

To show up for rehearsal -

A fiddler on the goof.

Old principals do

Not die, kids say, they merely

Lose their faculties.

Roundish teacher of

Math retires after lifetime

Conversant with pi.

Hat maker boards an

Old ferry, concerned with

This year's capsizes.

Poor girl meets rich guy,

Proposes, so anxious for

Her ceremoney.

Sheep ranchers harvest

Loads of wool for market, and

Profits are shear joy.

Hairdresser offers

Booze to all the women in

The beauty saloon.

Dermatologist

Tells patient that she needs to

Liquidate her skin.

Searched all over for

A coffee shop but did not

Have a latte luck.

Godfather has an

Apochryphal of cash that's

Weighing down his pants.

The patient calls

His neuropathy of the feet

Case of comatoes.

Pastries await cruise

Passengers debarking on

A dessert island.

He has always loved

His penne, in the present

As in the pasta.

Says his cough syrup

Is exceeding his fondest

Expectorations.

Biblical scholar

Sees my limp, says I need

Cane to be able.

Drama critic to

Shakespeare,"How do I love thee?

Let me count the plays."

So what if he had

A heart of stone, why did she

Take him for granite?

She fell deeply in

Love with her psychiatrist,

Hook, line and shrink her.

Defrauded soldier

Exchanges his uniform

For a civil suit.

Hating CIA,

He refuses to read those

Stories with despise.

Conductor of the

Symphony fouls up Mozart,

Goes into Haydn.

Called upon to read

His bar-mitzvah portion,

He was Torahfied.

Punch drunk from day long

TV, he was often called

The village videot.

Carpenter enters

Senior condo, says, "I gamed,

I sawed, I conga'd."

Some pigs avoided

This virus as these swine from

The other swine flew.

Bird lover at a

Nudist camp says she would play

With a cockatoo.

If a dentist is

Gay, does the child patient

Call him a tooth fairy?

Gynecologist

And proctologist post their

New orifice hours.

Takes shovel outside

After huge snowstorm and sees

It was of snow use.

Girl violinist lost

Her boyfriend, could no longer

Play without her beau.

Hated gardening

So much that cutting down twigs

Was shear agony.

Failing to win a

Music writing contest, he

Becomes score loser.

Upset on the job?

Start to scream, do not let boss

Reign on your tirade.

Have a body shop

To fix my car? Of course, I

Can wreck-o-mend one.

Judge sneezes into

Lawyer's face, says,

"So please recuse me."

Sir Lancelot sings to

His love Guenivere, "Knight and

Day, You Are the One."

Work ethic of a

Zealous cop: "Another day,

Another collar."

He says, "Let's get off

The dance floor." She replies, "Wait,

Just a minuet."

That screaming wretch was

Sixth of sextuplets, and is

The rant of the lot.

Musical update

Of Oliver Goldsmith's play,

"She Stoops to Conga."

Golfer would scream those

Four-letter words all the time,

Was par for the curse.

Vice squad closes beach

For nudies, proclaims to town:

No nudes is good nudes.

Modern teenagers

Update fairy tale: Snow White

And the Seven Dorks.

Who is in charge of

Animal heaven? Of course,

reigning cats and dogs.

Gargling to ease a

Painful throat demonstrates

Good deal of hoarse sense.

Child swallows some coins,

Is taken to hospital,

But doc finds no change.

Humpty Dumpty fell

Off the wall intact, but then

Scrambled away fast.

"I need to get my

Pants enlarged by next week's dance."

"Make Believe Ballroom?"

Gentleman butcher

Likes to sell his viands with

A gorgeous cape on.

Here they call the game soccer,

But in Europe they

Call the game footbrawl.

Casanova scored

With many girls, was he a

Noble or layman?

Lepidopterist

Joins army, eats in mess hall,

Sees the butter fly.

Hungry guests circle

Baby boy while the mohel

Readies the bris kit.

Soprano books cruise

To see if she can handle

Cuisine with high C's.

Movie comic sings to

His curvaceous co-star, "Thanks

For the Mammaries."

Captain Kidd assures

His cold crew that many days

Will be bootyful.

Male clothes horse

Flies to Asia to purchase

Cravats in Thailand.

Old Russian Commies

Met for dinner, cried "We were

Hungry, Soviet."

Some folks say we are

In the land of the fee and

The home of the knave.

Weather forecaster

Promises sunshine, turns out

To be a snow job.

British dentist sued

By man who claims his London

Bridge is falling down.

School sends kids to eye

Doc, returns them to class as

Dilated pupils.

Census Bureau hires

Thousands of workers to count

The copulation.

Know Democrats who

Are republicans, Republicans

Who are democrats?

"He was so cheap with

His girl friend that he

Would not give a wrap.

"Agricultural

Chief to address group on "The

State of the Onion."

"First I dream I'm a

Tepee, then a wigwam,."

Shrink says, "You're too tense."

Dorothy travels

To Chicago, sings."I'm Off

To See the Blizzard."

A drummer laments:

"I fell on my head and I

Suffered percussion."

In tennis singles,

See a court, net, tennis ball

And two racketeers.

Dentist to swim champ

Patient: "No lead in your teeth,

Just go for the gold."

Ice skating champion

Brags he is also a gay

Blade with his partners.

Swarovski explained

His process until his thoughts

Became crystal clear.

"Whenever he caught

A big one, fisherman sang

A happy tuna.

Asking his shrewish

Wife for his favorite dish,

He begs, "Quiche me, Kate."

"Exxon-Mobil boss

Applauds year-end profits with

"Oil's well that ends well."

"Have a taste of my

New prune ice cream." "Please don't do

Me any flavors."

Seated for dinner

In cafe, florist asks for

Bread and butter cups.

Indian women

Fighting over clothes in store

Ask, "Who's sari now?"

A Shakespearian

Actor willing to perform

In any hamlet.

Geezers refuse to

Travel abroad, prefer

Stay in continent.

Has fierce no-win spat

With his frigid wife, fears he's

Facing a stale mate.

Baker tries baking

A pumpernickel, but at

Once it goes a-rye.

Photojournalist

Excites her wide readership

With her prints charming.

Londoner being

Sued engages the support of

A good bannister.

Ball playing prostate

Sufferers decide to form

A leak of ther own.

Socialite goes to

Beauty shop and asks for a

Hairdo to dye for.

Do not climb up that

Volcano, for you could well

Fall down on your ash.

Exotic bird in

Jungle mates with another

Since toucan do it.

Remember that late

Great comedienne who starred

In "I Love Loosely"?

Mohawk ghosts return

To Halloween frights from their

Happy haunting grounds.

Fairy tale scribe writes

Tale of mayhem, but many

Folks find it too Grimm.

Mrs. Malaprop:

"For oral hygiene, rinse your

Mouth with some gargyle."

I woke up early,

Went to bathroom, and performed

My absolutions.

House of ill repute,

Reno, sits on acre of

Profitable raunch.

He finally jumps

Down to earth and now plays in

"Fiddler on the Stoop."

Mrs. Malaprop:

Don't eat sweets, you can become

A diabolic.

Sailor's girlfriend has

IBS, takes her on a

Slow bloat to China.

Rebel colonists

Would capture Redcoats. Cooks too

Would cacciatore.

He searched the world for

Mythic beasts, but frightened,

He kept dragon his feet.

Thief emerges from

Sewer hideout and admits

That grime does not pay.

Many folks favored

A health reform bill that had

A pubic option.

I'm cold on this golf course."

"Don't worry, I'll give you

A good handy cap."

Pugilist has job

Packing electronics, says

He's a good boxer.

Syrian carpet

Weaver achieves a life of

Rugs to riches.

"Where is your girl friend,

Mickey?" "In Disney Clinic

With a Minnie stroke."

If Madoff had lived

In Ottowa, would he have

Left canada dry?

Man with ED goes

To medical lab to take

Series of testes.

Football player takes

Sitz bath after being hit

Hard in the end zone.

Chinese restaurant

Boss calculates his profit

As just a dim sum.

Mrs. Malaprop:

If you catch the flu, try not

To get ammonia.

Inebriate shouts

That he wants to go shopping

At the nearest malt.

The plus-sized lady

Said she has been quite heavy

Since her first girthday.

The comic begins

His shtick. Loosen your buccals

And laugh your heads off.

Gung ho policeman,

In fresh uniform,

Is an arresting figure.

Luxury auto

Totalled by a truck, that's how

The Mercedes bends.

She: I want to hunt

For mistletoe. He: Kiss me

First, then take a bough.

Wealthy madame is

Surrounded by treasures and

Enjoys her copulence.

Ornithologist

Has girl friend who fears harm from

His new wood pecker.

Mrs. Malaprop:

The colors on her skirt seem

Like salt and peplum.

Madame in cat house:

This is the greatest fun since

The day I was porn.

At the concert hall,

Orchestra completes a long

Liszt of melodies.

Prom queen boasts that her

Brains and her chassis put her

Head of the classy.

A weathercaster

Needs to be friendly and have

Keen sense of humid.

Guitarist ignores

First offer from an agent,

Stringing him along.

Pilgrims used shellfish

As soil fertilizer, so

Went the lobster tale.

Mrs. Malaprop:

The cold cracked my window,

I called a glacier.

You really can win

That nudie beauty contest,

Just grin and bare it.

Expert maker of

Bicycle wheels, he is named

As firm's spokesperson.

Mrs. Malaprop:

Beware, boy, you could go blind

If you masticate.

He could not learn a

Foreign tongue because of his

Poor vowel movements.

Before flight into

Space, astronauts down some

Food at new lunching pad.

Inebriate drinks

Four bottles of scotch, is hauled

To court, pleads the fifth.

Sludge transport vessel

Posts a slogan on its bow:

Have gunk, will travel.

Did you like your trip

Through the State of Israel?"

"I loved it Eilat."

Boxers dance in the

Ring, close right in because it

Takes two to tangle.

Ruffian leaves farm,

Makes fortune in city, and

Returns to crass roots.

His skillful use of

Percussive instruments was

Cymbal of talent.

Ex-con becomes a

Coal miner, adjusting to

A new life of grime.

Health concerns lead to

Razing the hovel along

With the kitchen zinc.

The accused man would

Lie to the prosecutor,

Was court in the act.

Defense attorney

States that petty theft is bad,

But vice is versa.

So much nonsense talk

In kitchen that the baker

Could not folderol.

With no love for some

Amphibians, she waited

For the frog to croak.

Son of math teacher

Begs dad to please cosine

Loan application.

Trigonometry

Prof: Too few math students are

A sine of the times.

Famous baker's breads

Are well known in the far west

And in the near yeast.

Broadway comedy

Cast repeat their lines daily

By farce of habit.

His cows do not get

Pregnant, farmer feels he was

Given a bum steer.

Buyer to trader

Of fabric: "Don't dare pull the

Wool over my eyes."

Sometimes school programs

Seem like ridiculum in

The curriculum.

Democracy in

Cuba? When? Can those Castros

Be convertible?

My Jamaican guest

Enjoyed my kosher food,

And he did not dread lox.

Boy meets girl at dance

And immediately they

Fall madly in lust.

The new cantor in

My synagogue landed his

Well paid job by chants.

Those tipsy ballet

Dancers can hardly make it

To the next barre room.

Economy might

Grow when housing revives with

Only four closures.

Geezer decides to

Sue the hotel after he

Goes off his rocker.

He took Viagra,

They went to bed, and he rose

To the occasion.

Some folks against the

No Child Left Behind call it

A Blackboard Bungle.

As she listens all

Night to music, she shows signs

Of bulging eye pods.

Some think he's cute,

Others cite his revolting

Poisonality.

Couple leaves Chinese

Bistro singing "They Tried to

Sell Us Egg Foo Young."

CEO's: Cut out

The greed, and are you facing

A bonus onus?

No way to predict the

Movement of the stock market,

Finance seers don't know!

She works in sales for

Victoria's Secret,

Finds the job so uplifting.

Feuding factions of

Same party soon to attend

Annual contention.

Jailed language teacher

Expects wife's visit for a

Conjugating tryst.

Refusing to admit

He visited Egypt, he

Remained in deNile.

X-ray techs shun gas

Heat, prefer warmth of the old

Time radiation.

His pre-nup with rich

Gal, he explains, is a form

Of wife insurance.

Book of a convict's

Escape expected to be

A complete cellout.

Life, liberty, and

The pursuit of hippyness,

Cry of the sixties

She boards the huge ship

And for fifteen frantic nights

She enjoyed the crews.

Wedding couple beams

At their skyscraper cake in

All of its Splenda.

An actress, just cast,

Moves into new digs, grateful

What a part meant.

Senior citizens

Create own competition:

"Dancing With The Scars."

The magic in his

Dish designs was nothing short

Of sheer saucery.

Lawyer represents

Mugger's victim: we have here

An open and shut face.

Inebriate dad

Of a lisping son sends him

To a speakeasy.

"Did that film star win

Any award for acting?"

"Don't know, I'll Oscar."

TV breaking news:

Horny governors give up

Re-erection bids.

He told his buddies

That his wife's coffee might well

Be grounds for divorce.

Cleric crawls out of

Bed, goes to sink and performs

His absolutions.

Picks up heavyweight

Bride, filling groom with joy and

Uncommon rupture.

Mommy pig would not

Allow you to touch her, but

Would baby piglet?

Update: Jack and Jill

Went up the volcano and

Grabbed a piece of ash.

Anxious young woman

Attends Hawaiian luau,

Hopes for poi meets girl.